Front Cover:

Sgt. Alfred Burford returning home from Rangoon.

Back cover:

VE Day

Scottish Library Association
Motherwell Business Centre
Coursington Road
Motherwell ML1 1PW

© Scottish Library Association 1995

Newspaper extracts appear by
permission of their publishers.

ISBN 0 900649 93 3

Designed by GSB · Edinburgh
Photographs supplied by
"The Herald" and
Dumbarton District Libraries

Printed by Russell Print, Blantyre.

SMILING THROUGH

Yes! A Blighty, but still Smiling.

A Nurse from the Beaches said, "The wonderful Courage of the Men makes you want to cry, but *they* can always smile."

That's the Spirit of the Men who, on the soil of France, fight gallantly to free the world from Nazi Tyranny.

It is up to all of us at home to give them the assurance that we are with them all the way.

That assurance can be expressed by Saving More and More each Week for Victory.

SAVINGS STAMPS - - - - - - 6d, 2'6, and 5'-
SAVINGS CERTIFICATES - - - - 15'- and 20'-
Or Deposit in Post Office and Trustee Savings Banks.

Support the **INVASION**

Issued by the Scottish Savings Committee.

SCOTLAND
1945

EDITED BY
BRIAN D. OSBORNE
&
ROBERT CRAIG

SCOTTISH LIBRARY ASSOCIATION

1995

Clement Attlee and Winston Churchill

In January 1945 the Second World War in the West was well on the way to being won. There would still be much suffering and loss of life to be endured but as the New Year opened the western Allies had fought off the German counter-offensive in the Ardennes and were preparing to advance to the Rhine; in Italy Allied armies were fighting their way, against fierce German resistance, up through the Apennines; while on the Eastern Front the Russian Army was on the Vistula and poised to capture Poland and move on into eastern Germany. In the Far East the situation was much less hopeful and the prospect of a long and bloody conflict to defeat Japan, culminating in a costly invasion of the Japanese homeland, was pre-occupying the minds of politicians, military planners and the general public alike. The atomic bomb, which was to end the war in the East, was still an untested theory, a closely guarded secret and the largest scientific project in history.

On the Home Front the prospects of peace, and the return of military personnel was being keenly anticipated. Just as after the First World War there had been much enthusiasm for reconstruction and social change - the idea, for example, of "Homes fit for Heroes" - so in 1945 interest in social reform, in planning and in creating a new and better world from the ruins of the old was widespread.. Much of this concern for post-war planning had been encouraged by the Government whose war-time propaganda, co-ordinated by the Ministry of Information, had strongly emphasised the need for town planning, education and training, social welfare and housing. Total War had inevitably involved the state in the daily life of the citizen and this concern and involvement would continue into the peace.

In the midst of the war the all-party National Government had found time and resources to bring forward a large number of measures designed to cope with just this problem of post-war reconstruction. Measures such as the 1944 Education Act and the Beveridge Report of 1942, which laid the foundations for a comprehensive welfare state, addressed the social needs issues. The Town & Country Planning Act of 1945 gave a structure for comprehensive redevelopment of Britain's bomb-scarred towns and cities and sought to avoid the mistakes which had led to slums and pollution in the past. Entire New Towns were planned on greenfield sites away from the overcrowded cities and the origins of East Kilbride, Cumbernauld and Glenrothes are found in this zeal for planning. Even such a measure as the creation in 1943 of the North of Scotland Hydro-Electric Board was intended to help not only the industrial development of Scotland by providing electric power, but

VE Day

also its social welfare and the quality of life of its people.

These national concerns and initiatives found local reflection up and down Scotland and it is this local response to the pressures and changing circumstances of 1945 which forms the theme of this book. The demands of five years of war had called into being a great range of community based responses. Some were formal and statutory like the Auxiliary Fire Service, the Home Guard and the Air Raid Wardens. Others were informal and unofficial: one such expression of local solidarity were the Victory Clubs which came into existence in many towns and villages to raise money for End-of-War Funds and to plan homecoming gifts for servicemen and women.

The cost of the war, in soldiers, sailors and airmen being killed or wounded in action, captured or missing, was still being reported week by week in the local press. The hardships of the civilian population were to some extent reduced; the German Air Force was no longer in a position to mount bombing raids, although London and the South East of England would continue to suffer attacks by German V2 rockets until March 1945. However the lesser hardships of food rationing, fuel shortages, clothes rationing and homelessness were still all too unpleasantly present. In some cases these hardships would continue long after the coming of peace. Britain would have food rationing until 1954 and indeed 1946 would see the introduction of bread rationing - an extreme measure which had been avoided even at the worst period of the war. To an extent the prospects of peace made some problems worse - local authorities became concerned about the lack of housing for their returning soldiers and were anxious to build more homes and to recover houses which had been let to evacuees from blitzed communities.

One of the most obvious signs of the approach of peace was the resumption of normal political activity. The Conservative-led Coalition Government in power at the outbreak of war in September 1939 had in May 1940 been broadened into a National Government under Winston Churchill, with Conservative, Labour & Liberal ministers. A General Election would, in normal circumstances, have been due in 1940, but wartime conditions had made such an event impossible and undesirable. An electoral pact between the main parties had been agreed in 1939 and this had resulted in a suspension of party political activity. Any by-elections that had arisen had been dealt with by running an agreed National Government candidate drawn from the party which had previously held the seat, with only independents and minor party candidates providing opposition. In 1945 attention could again be spared for party politics and a General Election was held in July. As a preliminary to this the National Government resigned in May and the majority Conservative Party formed a caretaker administration under Churchill.

The election reflected the national mood for change and produced a landslide majority for Clement Attlee's Labour Party which won 393 seats compared to the Conservatives' 213. It might seem surprising, fifty years on, that the Prime Minister who had led the nation to victory and who, to many people, had symbolised the national spirit and national resistance during the darkest days of the war should have been so comprehensively rejected by the electorate. The explanations for this rejection vary but certainly there was a perception that Churchill might have been a great war-leader but was much less appropriate as an architect of post-war reform and reconstruction. Equally, the Conservative Party can be seen as paying the belated price for the economic troubles of the 1930s and for the pre-war policy of appeasing the fascist dictators. In any event the disruption, social change and suffering endured by the British people during six years of war probably made any notion of "business as usual" psychologically unpalatable. The injunction of the Conservative slogan "Send him back to finish the job" - that is re-electing a Churchill-led Conservative administration - fell on deaf ears.

These issues find expression in communities across Scotland, with particular shifts of emphasis depending on the character of the area, its local industries, the nature of its involvement with war-time work and the changes that peace might bring. In some cases one can see the Biblical vision of Isaiah "they shall beat their swords into plowshares and their spears into pruning hooks" being fulfilled. The Blackburn Aircraft Factory in Dumbarton stopped building warplanes and turned over to the production of pre-fabricated aluminium houses to meet the national housing shortage.

The difficult issues of resettlement, re-training, employment and housing for hundreds of thousands of demobilised service personnel and workers in war industries would prove a major concern. The impact of this can be seen in many parts of the country, sometimes given a special twist by the presence in local communities of prisoners of war living, it was sometimes claimed, in better conditions than the local population and undertaking work that returning servicemen saw as rightfully theirs. Women, who had been recruited in large numbers to traditionally male areas of employment, were laid off as the men returned from the forces.

The detailed picture of life in Scotland in 1945 that can be obtained from the nation's newspapers has, we believe, a real value in giving a local and a human dimension to the sometimes generalised or impersonal national and global perspective. The material available in libraries throughout the country, in newspaper files, archives, books and photographic collections, represents an invaluable asset to all those who would seek to know and to understand the past and to interpret the present. The editors are extremely grateful to colleagues throughout Scotland for their help and cooperation in the production of this book and also to the editors of the newspapers from which the extracts are taken for their permission to reprint. *Scotland 1945* is a sequel to an earlier Scottish Library Association publication – *Scotland 1939*. Together it is hoped that they give a valuable insight into Scotland at two critical points of change in its recent history. Teachers' Notes have kindly been prepared by Ronald Armstrong and will, we trust, enhance the value of *Scotland 1945* in schools. We hope, however, that this look at our country's past, from a local perspective, will be of interest to readers of all ages and stimulate a desire for further reading, investigation and reflection. ∎

COMRADES IN ARMS KILLED ON SAME DAY

News was received in Kirkintilloch this week of the death on active service in Europe of two local men - members of well-known families - who were friends in civilian life and comrades in arms in the same regiment - the Cameronians. The comrades who made the supreme sacrifice are Corporal William Ferrie...and Rifleman James D. McAlpine.

Corporal Ferrie, who is the second member of the Ferrie family to be killed in action in this war...joined the Forces in 1940.

Rifleman McAlpine, who is 36 years of age, was employed with the Forth & Clyde Steel Coy. before joining the Services in August 1940. He also is the second member of his family to be killed by enemy action in this war.

Kirkintilloch Herald 21st March 1945

ON LEAVE FROM BURMA

Driver Nicholas Rossi, Royal Corps of Signals, member of the well-known local family of restaurateurs, is on home leave from Burma. He joined the army early in the war and served in the Libyan campaign. Tobruk became as familiar to him as Motherwell. He saw it captured, defended, lost and recaptured.

Transferred to the eastern theatre of war, he was for a period in

Raising the Red Flag over the ruins of Berlin.

India before going on to Burma. Since he reached home he has been thrilled to hear that the 14th Army he knows so well and greatly admires is in Mandalay.

Motherwell Times 28th March 1945

DIED IN GERMAN PRISON CAMP

With so much talk last weekend of soldiers who were liberated coming home, and of the early prospects of many more local lads being liberated in the near future, not a few local parents have been very hopeful of receiving the joyful intimation that one of their loved ones would soon be homeward bound.

That is exactly how Mrs Elizabeth Geater...felt on Monday morning when the postman delivered an unusual official-looking letter and with the hope that her son, Richard, who had been captured at St. Valery* in June 1940 might have been liberated, she hurriedly opened the letter.

The news, however, was that Richard had died in Germany on March 3rd. "of Intestinal Occlusion".

Blantyre Gazette 7th April 1945
*The 51st Highland Division was encircled and forced to surrender at St. Valery in Normandy while covering the evacuation of British & French troops.

LENZIE'S WELCOME HOME FOR MAJOR ARMSTRONG

A wave of real joy and relief was felt throughout Lenzie last week when it became known that Major Jack Armstrong, son of Mrs Armstrong and the late Dr. Armstrong, and who had been a P.O.W.* in Germany for five years was on his way home...

He was at a camp beyond Kassel when American vanguards reached that city. The Germans forced their prisoners to march east away from the Americans, but the speedy advance of our Allies overtook the marching columns and brought about their release.

Kirkintilloch Herald 18th April 1945
*P.O.W. = Prisoner of War.

HOW LOCAL MAN WON M.M.

It has been announced that the Military Medal has been awarded to Private James Campbell Stewart, the Black Watch...for services on the North-West Front.

The citation states: "Pte. Stewart is a stretcher-bearer and has consistently carried out outstandingly good work in conveying casualties under fire...Pte. Stewart, with complete disregard for heavy machine-gun fire from infantry and tanks, moved out, tending the wounded and carrying them back on stretchers..."

Kirkintilloch Herald 9th May 1945

OPEN AIR TEA FOR 150

Baird's "top" Row last Friday evening presented a most unusual spectacle when the "neebors" went all out to provide an appropriate welcome home to Private Dick Cowan, of 25 Baird's Row, who arrived home earlier that day after having spent almost 5 years in German hands as a prisoner of war.

Long tables were placed along the roadway adjacent to the young soldier's home, and when tea was served, there were approximately 150 adult guests seated, full justice being done to the goodly array of eatables which mysteriously appeared. Despite extremely short notice the organisation of the function was admirably carried out by a capable committee of housewives representing the row - Mesdames Skelton, Murray, Gibson, and Robertson, who received most willing assistance from all the neighbours in securing and providing additional dainties for this feast...

Blantyre Gazette 12th May 1945

BRITISH TROOPS ARE IN BERLIN

British troops entered the western outskirts of Berlin in motorised columns at 3.30 yesterday afternoon.

Every soldier had the opportunity of voting in the British election before arrival in the city.

Aberdeen Press & Journal 5th July 1945

WARSHIPS STRIKE IN JAP WATERS

Allied warships and aircraft have

made daring thrusts far into the seas surrounding the home islands of Japan.

Shitsuka, river port on the south-east coast of Karafuto, most northerly Japanese territory, has been shelled by five American warships....

American aircraft are keeping up their round-the-clock attack on the Japanese islands.

Aberdeen Press & Journal 5th July 1945

ANOTHER HORROR CAMP DISCOVERED

A Nazi extermination factory, where hundreds of allegedly mentally deficient or deformed German women and children were still being destroyed has been discovered at Kaufburen, Bavaria, by American Army authorities.

The method of destruction was by intramuscular injections or slow starvation.

The chief nurse, who confessed that she had murdered "approximately" 220 children in two years by intramuscular injection, asked "Will anything happen to me?"

Aberdeen Press & Journal 5th July 1945

GESTAPO BLACK LIST FOR BRITAIN

The Gestapo* Black List of people in Britain wanted by the Nazis has been found in Berlin and published yesterday.

There are 2000 names on the list, ranging from Mr. Churchill and his cabinet to obscure German refugees.

Many well known figures in British public life were mentioned... About forty British newspapers and publications were also high on the list.

Inverness Courier 14th September 1945
*The German Secret Police.

BELSEN CAMP PICTURES FOR EXHIBITION

Photographs taken in the Belsen* horror camp will be available for inspection by adults only at the Thanksgiving Savings Week Exhibition which opens in the local Town Hall on Saturday afternoon. The exhibition promises to be one of the most ambitious and interesting of its kind, and citizens are asked to make a point of paying it a visit during the week.

Kirkintilloch Herald 3rd October 1945
*The Belsen Concentration camp, had been liberated by British troops in April 1945.

RELEASE FROM SERVICES

Owners of one-man businesses whose applications for release from the Services on compassionate grounds have been refused, can have their cases reviewed if they resubmit their applications. Those eligible to apply for release are men who carried on their own business before enlistment, or men whose father, mother or wife carried on a business without help, and the business is in danger of closing down because they are unable to continue.

Kirkintilloch Herald 3rd October 1945

REPATRIATED PRISONERS GIVEN GREAT WELCOME

A great reception was accorded on Sunday evening to the first two Newtongrange repatriated prisoners to have returned from the Far East. They were Lance Corporal Peter White Purves and Pte. Thomas McIntosh, of the Royal Scots, who were taken prisoner by the Japanese at the fall of Hong Kong. The former, who was a regular soldier, was making his first visit home in nearly eleven years. The Newtongrange Lothian and Juvenile Pipe Bands...met the men...and played them to their homes...Flags and bunting were flying from many houses on the route. Both were looking well following their long and gruelling experience in enemy hands.

Dalkeith Advertiser 1st November 1945

KIRKINTILLOCH MAN AT PALACE

Mr Robert Marshall, a chief engineer in the Merchant Navy, attended an Investiture at Buckingham Palace on Tuesday of last week, when he received the O.B.E. from the King. Chief Engineer Marshall was a member of the crew of the S.S. Rathlin, which was noted for its work as a rescue ship in convoys. The ship made numerous trips in the Murmansk convoy run, and was attacked very frequently by enemy 'planes...

Also present at this investiture was Group Captain Bader, the famous legless "ace" of Fighter Command. He

Paper thrown from windows in Regent Street following Japanese surrender.

received the bar to the D.S.O. and the bar to the D.F.C.

Kirkintilloch Herald 5th December 1945

HOME GUARD STANDS DOWN

The Home Guard* is to be disbanded on December 31, 1945, when members will cease to be liable to recall and the uniform which they have been authorised to retain will become their personal property, the War Office announces. A district man who has continued to give the Home Guard as his excuse for going out on certain evenings of the week will not welcome the publication of the above.

Kirkintilloch Herald 19th December 1945

*The Home Guard had been established (as the Local Defence Volunteers) in May 1940 to help guard against threatened invasion.

Queue for vegetables

CUT IT OUT GIRLS!
Local Soldier's Opinion of the Italians

Another of our readers who gets his "Gazette" as regularly as circumstances will permit, and who is at present "Somewhere in Italy" ...tells us his opinion of the Italian prisoners in this country...and of the girls who go out of their way to seek their company.

Here is what Gunner McKenzie says:

"All the boys out here have read with contempt the manner in which the Eyties[1] are being treated back home - especially the way the lassies seem to be attracted by them.

"Well, all we out here have to say is that those same lassies should have been in Africa for a spell when possibly some of their fathers, brothers or sweethearts were fighting the Italians. They were all-powerful then and showed us no mercy, with the aid of their friends the Huns[2].

"Then after El Alamein[3], they should have seen the same Italians run...

"I hope some of these lassies will pack up these flirtations with the Italian prisoners. Surely there are plenty of Tommies[4] about who would be better company - or are all the Tommies over here?"

Blantyre Gazette 6th January 1945

[1]. Eyties = slang term for Italians
[2]. Huns = slang term for Germans
[3]. Battle of El Alamein, October 1942.

British forces under General Montgomery defeated German & Italian forces under Field Marshall Rommel.

[4]. Tommy = British soldier. From use of name "Thomas Atkins" on specimen Army pay-book.

CIGARETTES GIFT FOR MEN ON LEAVE

First gesture to local men of the B.L.A.* coming home on leave was made at the week-end by the Kirkintilloch Victory Club, who intimated that 50 cigarettes would be issued to each man on presentation of his leave pass.

Kirkintilloch Herald 10th January 1945

* B.L.A.= British Liberation Army - British troops in North West Europe.

LETTERS TO THE EDITOR
Reputation Tarnished

Sir - If all reports are true, Kirkintilloch's cherished reputation for showing kindness to the stranger in our midst was tarnished last week by the action of a number of youths in assaulting a coloured Service man outside a hall. This coloured lad is but one of many hundreds who have travelled thousands of miles to help Britain in her hour of grave peril, and to be repaid in this fashion is surely ingratitude in its worst form....Surely if one must fight - and there are numerous opportunities for doing so in Europe and in Italy and Burma - it should be with, and not against our Allies... Yours, etc. "Ex-Serviceman"

Kirkintilloch Herald 10th January 1945

RATION REGULATIONS CONTRAVENED

At the Edinburgh Sheriff Court on Monday, a fine of £10 was imposed on William Steven, baker...Dalkeith, who admitted contravening the Food Ration Regulations by having a quantity of lard in excess of the amount allowed.

Dalkeith Advertiser 25th January 1945

SHORTAGES AFFECT ALL THE FAMILY

At a local dance the other evening baby's "dummies" were given as prizes in one competition. At the close there was an enquiry by a party very anxious to procure a "dummy" for a friend's baby. These "dummies" are in short supply at the moment.

Kirkintilloch Herald 7th March 1945

FURNACES IDLE AT DALZELL
Serious Effect of Coal Shortage

As a result of the fuel shortage 11 steel-making furnaces and several mills ceased operations on Wednesday at the Dalzell Works of Colvilles Ltd., and 2000 employees have been notified that seven days from the date of the stoppage their employment with the Company will be terminated.

Motherwell Times 9th March 1945

CLYDEBANK EVACUEES IN COUNCIL HOUSES

Kirkintilloch Town Council, with a big waiting list for Council houses, are anxious to recover those let to evacuees from Clydebank*, ... [and has requested] that Clydebank Town Council should give special consideration to evacuees from their area who were occupying Town Council houses in Kirkintilloch, so that these houses could be made available to applicants in this burgh, many of whom were living in insanitary and overcrowded conditions.

Kirkintilloch Herald 14th March 1945

1. Clydebank had been attacked in a major air-raid or blitz in March 1941 which killed over 500 people and destroyed or damaged beyond repair 4,300 homes.

WELFARE FOODS SCHEME

In the course of her address [at Blantyre] Mrs Lincoln said that the infant death rate might be expected to rise during war - work and worry for mothers, rationing, etc., but it had fallen from 57 to 50 per 1000 in England and Wales and in Scotland from 77 to 65 per 1000. The reason was better feeding, and particularly the welfare foods scheme. We want more consumption of welfare foods and less illness and death among babies. Orange juice and cod liver oil contained necessary vitamins to ensure that babies had a proper start in life.

Blantyre Gazette 24th March 1945

VE Day decorations being erected in Perth

BEVIN BOYS NOT IN UNION
Miners Go On Strike

The day shift at Whitehill Pit of the Lothian Coal Company at Rosewell struck work on Saturday in connection with a dispute which has arisen as a result of the employment of some 40 Bevin boys*...

The local Pit Committee recently appealed to the lads to join the Miners' Union, but many of them explained that they did not intend to follow mining work as a vocation in peace time, and would be seeking other employment as soon as they were released by the Government.

Being averse to the employment of non-union workers the miners accordingly went on strike on Saturday as a protest. As a consequence there was a loss of output amounting to 500 tons of coal...the intention is to repeat the one day a week strike until the Bevin boys and other trainees are persuaded to join the Union.

Dalkeith Advertiser 5th April 1945

*Bevin Boys were young men, frequently from non-mining backgrounds, conscripted into coal-mining as an alternative form of National Service to the Armed Forces. Named after Ernest Bevin (1881-1951) Minister of Labour & National Service in the wartime Coalition Government.

THE MULBERRY HARBOUR

Warm congratulations to Lanarkshire workers for their important contribution to the making of the Mulberry* harbour were extended by Rear Admiral H. Hickling, CBE, DSO, who had charge of the construction of the harbour on the Normandy beaches, when he paid a visit to Messrs Alex. Findlay & Co's. Parkneuk Works at Motherwell on Wednesday.

Rear Admiral Hickling said he was particularly glad to visit these works and to meet the men and women who had done such a good job, working by day and by night to produce key parts for the Mulberry harbour, without the incentive of knowing what they were working for. The whole success of the invasion depended on the "Mulberry" and without it they could have had no guarantee that the vital supplies for our armed forces could have been landed....

Of the 23 pierheads in the Mulberry 18 were constructed by this firm...

Motherwell Times 11th April 1945

*Mulberry was the code name for pre-fabricated artificial harbours which were used on the Normandy invasion beaches until Allied forces could gain control of French ports.

COAL RATIONING

In most households it has for long now been a considerable struggle to make the limited amount of coal allowed spin out for the prescribed period. The task will not be any easier as a result of being reduced to a maximum of four hundredweights* for the month of April....There is little prospect of coal allowances being

Steeling a march! Trust Gillette's fine-tempered edge to get through where the going's toughest. On the Elbe or on the chin, Gillette in battledress smooths the way—to that *victory smile*! Gillette in battledress, maybe—but Gillette true to form!

Gillette in battledress

"Standard" Gillette Blades (plain steel) 2d each, including Purchase Tax. Fit all Gillette razors, old or new.
If you can't always get them, remember they're worth trying for! Production still restricted.

increased during the summer months, so that it looks as if everybody will be rather hard put to it to build up any stock of fuel for next winter.

Dalkeith Advertiser 19th April 1945
*Approximately 200 kilograms.

"SPUDS" SCARCE

Potatoes were...in short supply in Kirkintilloch during the early part of last week, and in many homes there were "spudless" dinners. The situation was eased somewhat towards the end of the week, when supplies arrived.

Kirkintilloch Herald 9th May 1945

LETTERS TO THE EDITOR
The 'Bus Strike

Sir - While on leave at my home last week I was very disgusted to learn of the 'bus strike involving several employees of Messrs Lawson's Ltd. There is nothing which makes we members of

H.M. Forces, both in this country and other lands, more discontented than to be repeatedly hearing of strikes which occur in so many parts of the British Isles. It would be a very sad day for Great Britain if the Royal Navy, Army and Royal Air Force went on strike for one day... Continual strikes of this nature cause a rapid decrease in the production of armaments which are very necessary for a successful conclusion to the war with Japan. Shame on you, drivers and 'bus conductresses.

Yours etc. "Disgusted ATS Corporal"

Kirkintilloch Herald 9th May 1945

TEACHERS COMPLAIN ABOUT COLD SCHOOLS

A deputation from the Lanarkshire Association of the Educational Institute of Scotland was received by the Education Committee in connection with the recent decision to discontinue heating in schools after the Easter holidays.

Lanarkshire, as far as could be ascertained, was the only area in Britain in which there had been a heating ban this year. Owing to the operation of Double Summer Time, children were really attending school at 7am, a time when at this period of the year, even under normal conditions, temperatures were generally low. Conditions in the schools had been the subject of complaints and protests from all over the County, and their experience of conditions at the beginning of this week had convinced them that some modification of the regulation regarding heating was urgently necessary.

Hamilton Advertiser 3rd May 1945

RESETTLEMENT ADVICE

In connection with the Government's Demobilisation scheme which comes into operation next month, four special Resettlement Advice Offices are to be opened soon in Lanarkshire by the Ministry of Labour. At these centres advice will be given to demobilised men and women on personal problems and on all questions dealing with their return to civilian life.

Hamilton Advertiser 21st May 1945

ADVERTISEMENT
CLOSING OF AIR RAID SHELTERS

Notice is hereby given that all Public and Communal Domestic Shelters provided by the County Council will be considered closed on and after 3rd June 1945. Any householders who have installed furnishings in them should arrange to remove them immediately.

Kirkintilloch Herald 30th May 1945

JITTERBUG CONTEST

The first Jitterbug Contest to be held in Peebles took place in the Drill Hall on Tuesday evening, when 5 couples took part.

South Midlothian Advertiser 15th June 1945

VJ celebrations in Perth High Street

MINEFIELDS DISRUPT HOLIDAYS

Minefields are being cleared as rapidly as possible around the north-east coast of Scotland. It is not a task that can be rushed and holidaymakers will not have unrestricted use of all beaches and foreshores this summer.

Aberdeen Press and Journal 17th July 1945

MORE ABSENTEEISM IN ABERDEEN YARDS

"There seems to be an end-of-the-war feeling abroad. The tendency to take a little more than the official holiday is definitely on the increase in our experience," a representative of one establishment told "The Press and Journal".

A shipyard manager said..."We still have a number of high priority jobs to carry out to help win the war against Japan. In fact we are still working three nights a week overtime and working on every second Sunday."

Aberdeen Press and Journal 24th July 1945

DALKEITH SCHOOLBOYS HELP WITH FRUIT HARVEST

Some Dalkeith school boys will not be grieved if they do not see a raspberry again for a long time. They are members of a party of High School senior pupils who spent a month of their holidays helping with the berry picking in Perthshire....

The raspberries were put in "luggies" or small pails, tied to the picker's waist. These receptacles held a few pounds and when they were full they were emptied into big containers at the end of the rows. A good average forenoon's picking was about 20lbs....

In the district it had been considered that boys were not suitable for berry picking, girls being thought better, but the Dalkeith boys disproved this theory.

Dalkeith Advertiser 23rd August 1945

CHANNEL ISLANDS EVACUEE

Over four years ago a bright, smart, little lad, Master Cecil Le Mesuirier, an evacuee from the Channel Islands, came to reside in our village [Torrance]. His foster parents were Mr

& Mrs John Semple, of Viola Place. He was much attached to all he came in contact with and made many friends during his stay with us...On Tuesday he left us to go back to his mother, whom he has not seen for four years...The good wishes of the whole community goes with Cecil for all joy and happiness in the great reunion. He has taken with him a bunch of heather, but best of all, he has acquired a fine Scots accent, and his mother, we are afraid, will require an interpreter.

Kirkintilloch Herald 5th September 1945

ROW OVER GERMANS

After one of its stormiest meetings...Lanarkshire County Council agreed to employ German P.O.W. labour for the preparation of housing sites.

Members spoke of their frank disbelief of Ministry of Labour assertions that no other labour is available.

The trouble started when a Ministry of Labour figure was quoted suggesting that there wasn't sufficient Scottish labour, and that German prisoners of war should be engaged...

Mr Beechcroft...gave a description of Argylls, Black Watch men and Cameronians, etc. lining up at "buroos"* while Germans worked on housing.

Blantyre Gazette 8th September 1945
*Buroo = bureaux = Employment Exchange.

STEPNEY ADOPTION SCHEME

It will be remembered that the bombed-out people of Stepney were adopted by the Northern area of the W.V.S. Gifts and money subscriptions were received last spring from members and their friends from Nairn to Caithness... Mrs Gooch, W.V.S. District Administrator for the Northern Area has now heard that 2300 families have been re-equipped in Stepney, in all about 11,794 people. The process has been slow owing to the difficulties of actually re-housing the people.

Inverness Courier 14th September 1945

WOMEN IN WAR WORK

A very successful re-union and farewell party was held in the canteen of Anderson, Boyes & Co. Ltd on Saturday. The occasion was a party...for the women and girls from the factory who had already left the factory and the girls who are now redundant owing to male labour replacing female labour.

Mr Anderson (Managing Director) said "I do not think sufficient has been said in public about the wonderful job that the factory girls have accomplished during the war. Neither their jobs nor their uniforms have had the glamour or the excitement of the girls who manned anti- aircraft batteries or Radar outposts, but their job has just been as vital and has been accomplished with the same exactitude and devotion to duty.

"Perhaps the nation's experience during the last six years will have brought forward for future generations to note the valuable characteristics which our women folk have demonstrated anew."

Motherwell Times 28th November 1945

WELCOME SIGNS

Welcome signs of pre-war days are to be seen in Dalkeith and Bonnyrigg these past few weeks. For the first time since war began, shops are beginning to take on something of their pre- war stock. Memories of bygone days were renewed the other evening when I dropped in at a number of well-known business premises which had recently acquired their Christmas goods. Though these were not of the same standard - both in quality and quantity - as 1939, they were nevertheless a big jump ahead of our war-time limits.

Soon, it is hoped, fairy lights will once again decorate the windows of local shops and even happier memories will be restored.

Dalkeith Advertiser 29th November 1945

RADIO FAVOURITES

For several years now the Rosewell folk have never failed to provide a good audience at the weekly Wireless Discussion Group held in Rosewell School on Monday evenings. During war years this little group, where one can express his or her opinions as to the wireless

VE celebrations in George Square, Glasgow.

programmes, has proved to be an excellent pastime for the winter evenings.

Dalkeith Advertiser 13th December 1945

WOOL FOR COMFORTS

Mrs Haldane, Lingerwood House, has received a consignment of wool from Comfort Headquarters for socks for those serving in the Far East and European zones. The need for socks by Service personnel is very urgent... Anyone in the village willing to knit socks on behalf of these men are asked to communicate with Mrs Haldane, who will distribute the necessary wool.

Dalkeith Advertiser 20th December 1945

A BANANA

An awed silence melted the hubbub of the hospital ward. Dragging my fixed stare from this treasure, I met a concentrated barrage of disbelieving eyes all focussed with shocked rigidity upon my prize.

After six long years I had resumed an old friendship, and as I reflectively scoured the recesses of my teeth with tentative tongue, I concluded that nature - in-the-raw - in the divine form of a banana - was certainly a bountiful blessing.

Dalkeith Advertiser 20th December 1945

Street party VE Day

V-E DAY CELEBRATIONS

Flood-lighting of the Municipal Offices will be a feature of Hamilton's celebrations to mark the end of the war in Europe. The buildings will be illuminated on the night of V-E day[1]...

Public-houses in the town will be open only during the usual hours for the sale of excisable liquor, and even then only if supplies last sufficiently long....

Churches in the town will be open for short services, and it is hoped that church bells will be rung[2]...

Hamilton Advertiser 5th May 1945

[1]. V-E Day = Victory in Europe Day. Eventually observed on Monday 8th May 1945.

[2]. In the event of an invasion church bells were to be rung to give warning. As a result their normal use had been forbidden until the coming of peace.

V-DAY SIGNAL HAILED WITH QUIET JOY

The North east and North of Scotland celebrated the Victory and the Peace yesterday in a spirit of thanksgiving and quiet joy, symbolised by the pealing of kirk bells in city, town and village and rural countryside.

Thousands went to the churches which were open for prayer, and there were family gatherings round most hearths to listen to the King.

Along the coast, fishing vessels' whistles were sounded after the Premier's announcement of the end of hostilities. At Peterhead the maroons used for calling out the lifeboat crew were fired.

Away from the coastal strip bonfires blazed last night on many a hill.

Throughout the area public buildings, business premises and dwellings were all beflagged, and in the harbour the boats flew buntings and pennants.

Generally the day was observed as a holiday, as to-day will be, and the schools remained closed.

Aberdeen Press & Journal 9th May 1945

ROSEWELL VICTORY CELEBRATIONS

There was a spontaneous outbreak of rejoicing in Rosewell when

Street party VE Day

news came through on Monday night that Germany had surrendered to the Allies. Flags and bunting quickly appeared on most houses, and there was some dancing in the streets. An attractive sight was presented at the pithead baths which were beautifully floodlit. There was a thanksgiving service in both the Parish Church and the St. Matthew's Church on Tuesday evening. A late night dance was held by the Anti-Gloom Campaigners.*

Dalkeith Advertiser 10th May 1945

*The Anti-Gloom Campaigners were a group of local residents who, during the war years, had organised fund raising entertainments for the village.

ATOMIC REPERCUSSIONS

The Town Goes Gay on Japanese Defeat

The blast of the atomic bomb[1] must surely be only as a little puff of wind compared to the effects of the few words spoken by the Prime Minister at midnight on Tuesday.

The tension of the previous three or four days was being overcome by most folks, and, content in the knowledge that it was only a matter of time before the Japanese were compelled to accept the Potsdam Declaration[2], they went to their bed at their accustomed time.

Not everyone, however, and when the gladdening news was officially proclaimed the streets of the district were suddenly filled with hurrying people, all going to break the news to friends and relatives.

Blantyre Gazette 18th August 1945

[1]. The dropping of atomic bombs on Hiroshima (6th August) and Nagasaki (9th August) had led to the Japanese surrender on 14th August. 160,000 people were killed or injured in the Hiroshima blast.

[2]. The main allied powers (Britain, Soviet Union & United States) met in July 1945 at Potsdam in the Crimea to settle the structure of the post-war world. Among their decisions was an insistence on the unconditional surrender of Japan, although it was known that the Japanese were seeking a negotiated peace.

DALKEITH PIPER PLAYS IN THE FIRST DAY OF PEACE

News of Japan's surrender was cordially received in Dalkeith and district, from where many men are still in the Far East and have long been at grips with the enemy. To their parents, wives and relatives the news of the end of the Far East war would be particularly pleasing.

The news for which the world had been eagerly waiting for some days earlier came in a midnight broadcast by the Prime Minister on Tuesday of last week. Mr Attlee was then able to announce that Japan had surrendered and the last of our enemies laid low. So ended for the British people six years of trial and endurance. It is a glorious finish and one which will everlastingly redound to the honour of our armed forces and to the men and women at home who resolutely put their shoulder to the wheel through the darkest days of the war and refused to contemplate defeat...

Piper Thomas Forrest, a veteran Dalkeith piper, added his contribution to the afternoon's proceedings, when, in full Highland garb, he marched round the streets at the head of a procession of children, many of whom had donned fancy dress....

Towards ten o'clock the crowds drifted towards White Hart Street, where the celebrations reached their peak...

...there was a huge gathering present when Provost Lean opened this culminating part of the V-J* day celebrations. The Provost...said:

"We have waited a long, long six years for this night, and it gives me great pleasure to take part in the proceedings. Like most pleasures, however, it is somewhat tinged with sadness, because in the midst of our revelry don't let us forget that this victory has been bought at a terrible price.

"It has cost the Allied Nations six million men, dead and wounded...let us for a moment think of the price we have paid and also think for a few seconds of the fathers and mothers who have given up their sons to make your revelry possible at all."

Dalkeith Advertiser 23rd August 1945

*V-J Day = Victory in Japan Day. Celebrated on 15th August 1945.

Crowds outside Downing Street cheering Mr Attlee.

END OF COALITION

Mr. Johnston, Secretary of State for Scotland, said in his address to the delegates that the war would end this summer and that political warfare would be soon thereafter in the full and open blast. He was not sure but that in the chaotic and difficult times that lay ahead for everybody, it would have paid the country better had we been able to maintain national unity for some time longer, and he was not sure but that many people who were at present so eager on both sides sharpening the swords of political partisanship would live to regret their excess of zeal. Be that as it might, there were great domestic issues like "housing, health and the right to work" that he hoped would in the interest of their own folk and the folk of every party be kept as far as possible outside the arena of partisan strife. They must never get back to the awful days of mass unemployment in the industrial belt of Scotland.

Kirkintilloch Herald 14th March 1945

TOM JOHNSTON STANDS DOWN

The end of the present political Coalition means the end of Mr. Tom Johnston's term as Secretary of State for Scotland. As Mr. Johnston is not to seek re-election to Parliament, the people of Scotland will be losing the services of one who is generally agreed to be the best Secretary of State the country has ever had the good fortune to possess. Mr. Johnston, in his smaller sphere, duplicated the triumph of Mr. Churchill as leader of the Government.

Kirkintilloch Herald 30th May 1945

THE CAMPAIGN TRAIL

Coming back to Britain in the hour of victory and with our tails up we are astonished to find an attitude of defeatism. We find that there is talk of woe and calamity. At a time when the prestige of this country is at its highest we find a lot of mud slinging going on with certain people preaching a rotten gospel aimed at getting rid of Churchill. It is absolutely wrong. In this election scrap six million men and women under the age of 31 will be voting for the first time. Most of us have heard throughout our lives of little else but wars and the troubles that arise from wars. Why is this?

To blame the system or a party is sheer nonsense. Most of the blame is with Germany and the Hun warmongers.

Speech by Lord Lovat, Commando Leader and Joint Under Secretary at the Foreign Office

Aberdeen Press and Journal 3rd July 1945

CAMPAIGN TRAIL

The final rally in the General Election brought many distinguished speakers to the town. Mr. Ernest Bevin outlined briefly the Labour Party policy with special emphasis for the mines. He said that the Government had paid the landowners £66,000,000 for the pits since war broke out and added that if the coal industry question was not settled satisfactorily, nothing would stop this country from having long queues of unemployed as we had before the war.

South Midlothian Advertiser 13th July 1945

LABOUR'S GREAT SUCCESS IN GENERAL ELECTION

The General Election results declared on Thursday, with a few still to come, gave the Labour Party a total of 390 seats in the new House of Commons. They have gained over two hundred seats, mostly from Conservatives, with only four losses, and have secured a majority of 153 over all other parties and groups.

Hamilton Advertiser 28th July 1945

ELECTION SENSATION

In many homes the radio was on from morning to night. Sensation after sensation came over the wavelengths as news came in of the amazing landslide in favour of Labour.

Kirkintilloch Herald 1st August 1945

CHURCHILL DEFEATED

Broadcasts on election result day made it clear that Labour had won a bigger victory throughout the

Housewife votes in Glasgow.

Above: Clement Attlee on the campaign trail at Falkirk. Right: Outside Buckingham Palace the King congratulates Clement Attlee on becoming Prime Minister

country than anyone had ever dreamed of. Britain had undergone a silent revolution.

The chief lesson of the Government defeat is that the British people will not be dominated by one man. They universally admire Mr. Churchill as a Great Englishman; they are grateful to the war leader, but they are resentful of the party politician. Mr. Churchill's broadcasts and his effort to turn the election into a personal plebiscite must have done him much harm. The efforts of Lord Beaverbrook were actually a disservice to the Tories and the soldier's vote in particular went against them.

Kirkintilloch Herald 8th August 1945

SELF GOVERNMENT FOR SCOTLAND

Speaking at a meeting in Motherwell Dr. McIntyre said that many of the votes cast at the recent election in Scotland were for candidates who were pledged to support a measure of self-government for Scotland. The National Party held, however, that it was not just a question of devolution and the setting up of a glorified County Council in Edinburgh which was of importance to Scotland. "We assert that Scotland is a nation and that her citizens have certain inalienable rights to a free life".

Motherwell Times 10th August 1945

NCB flag hoisted at Douglas Castle Colliery after nationalisation.

ALLIED DESTRUCTION OF THE ENEMY'S TRANSPORT SYSTEM PAVED THE WAY TO VICTORY, BUT WITHOUT TRANSPORT IT WAS IMPOSSIBLE TO DISTRIBUTE FOOD EVENLY. BOMBED BRIDGES AND BATTERED RAILWAYS ADDED TO THE GROWING SHORTAGE OF FOOD. A FEW AREAS HAD PLENTY — OTHERS STARVED — A FORETASTE OF THE PROBLEM FACING THE WORLD TO-DAY.

EUROPE'S CHILDREN NEED CLOTHES NOW

A circular from WVS headquarters emphasises the need for clothing especially warm underclothing for the children of Europe and gives the following facts. In Czechoslovakia clothing is mostly manufactured from artificial fibres; In France, newborn children are wrapped in newspapers; In Greece thousands of children are dressed in thin rags; while in Norway many will die due to being underclothed.

Kirkintilloch Herald 2nd May 1945

HIMMLER COMMITS SUICIDE

Heinrich Himmler, the infamous Gestapo Chief, committed suicide while being searched at British Second Army Headquarters at Luneburg at 11 o'clock on Wednesday night. He crushed a tiny phial of potassium cyanide between his teeth while a doctor was examining his mouth and managed to swallow it despite efforts by the doctor and Army officers to prevent him.

On May 21st British troops stopped him in disguise west of Hamburg. He was in civilian clothes, wearing a patch over one eye and had shaved off his moustache.

Thus ingloriously died one who of all the Nazi gang inspired the greatest fear and hatred and was the incarnation of their creed of calculated cruelty and bestiality.

Inverness Courier Friday 25th May 1945

Clement Attlee, Harry Truman and Joseph Stalin at Potsdam.

EUROPE - FOOD CUTS IN GERMANY

The maximum food allowance for German manual labourers is to be reduced by 1200 calories per day in view of the gravity of the food situation in the Rhine Valley and Western half of the Ruhr. The allowance will amount to about one-third of the quantity given to manual labourers in Britain.

Inverness Courier
29th May 1945

ALLIED CONTROL OF BERLIN

A communique issued yesterday afternoon after the first meeting of the Allied Control Council in Berlin, stated that agreement had been reached on a separate zone in Greater Berlin for the forces of France. So far France has administered part of the British sector, now she is to have her own area.

Inverness Courier
21st July 1945

FOOD FACTS

Nourishing High Tea and SUPPER DISHES

There's a real art in serving the right sort of last meal, whether it's High Tea or Supper, especially in wartime. It should be well-balanced, satisfying but not stodgy, and sufficiently nourishing to repair the day's wear and tear on nerves and tissues. It should include either a raw salad or correctly cooked vegetable dish, and one of the body-building foods: cheese, dried egg, bacon, meat or fish; with bread, cake or scone as 'fillers'.

Here are some High Tea and Supper recipes that win on all counts. Try them and see how well they go down.

A COMPLETE MENU

Salmon Savoury. Watercress & Beetroot Salad, Bread, Margarine, Jam or Marmalade

SALMON SAVOURY

Ingredients: 4 level tablespoons flour, quarter pint water, 3 heaped tablespoons salmon (quarter lb.), ¼ teaspoon mixed herbs, 1 teaspoon vinegar, salt and pepper. *Quantity:* Enough for 4. *Method:* Mix flour with a little of the water, bring remainder of water to boiling point, add to flour paste and allow to boil for 5 minutes. Then add salmon, herbs, vinegar and seasoning to taste, Pour on to slices of toast and place under a grill for 2 minutes. Serve with salad of beetroot and watercress. To finish the meal, serve bread and margarine, with jam or marmalade.

YOU'LL ENJOY THIS!

A recipe that is "different":

SOUR-SWEET CABBAGE
with Sausage-meat Cakes

Ingredients: 1 lb. cabbage, 1½ level teaspoons salt, 1 oz. bacon fat or dripping, 6 tablespoons vinegar, 1 level tablespoon jam or sugar, 2-3 cloves, 1 lb. sausage meat. *Method:* Cook the cabbage in a little boiling salted water till tender. Strain. Boil the bacon fat, or dripping, with the vinegar, jam or sugar and cloves for several minutes. Strain, and pour over the cooked cabbage. Serve with sausage meat divided into cakes, and fried slowly on both sides till cooked through.

NOTE ON POTATOES

While potatoes are scarce, use the utmost care to avoid waste in preparation. If the potatoes are small and not too old they are much better boiled in their skins. This saves time and trouble and retains the full flavour.

Rinse out Milk Bottles, and return DAILY.

THIS IS WEEK 40 — THE LAST WEEK OF RATION PERIOD No. 10 (April 1st to April 28th)

THE MINISTRY OF FOOD, LONDON, W.I. FOOD FACTS No. 251

QUISLING'S TRIAL OPENS

The trial of Vidkun Quisling, the puppet premier of Norway under the German occupation began in Oslo yesterday. He was accused of direct, premeditated and treasonable co-operation with the Germans, among other charges which included manslaughter, violation of the Constitution, improper use of public funds and even stealing silver from the Royal Palace.

Inverness Courier 11th August 1945

STARVING EUROPE

An appeal has been issued by the Bishop of Chichester and others calling attention to danger of mass starvation in Europe and, in particular, to the plight of millions of Germans expelled from their homes in Eastern Germany. It is reckoned that there are 13,000,000 for whom there is no food immediately available.

Hamilton Advertiser 13th October 1945

The first batch of 'Prefabs' outside the factory in Dumbarton.

TEMPORARY HOUSES

In a circular from the Department of Health it was stated that arrangements had been made by the Government to accelerate considerably the production and availability to local authorities of temporary houses. Under these arrangements delivery of temporary houses in Scotland was expected to commence in February, 1945 and to continue in increasing numbers in succeeding months.

Dalkeith Advertiser 11th January 1945

HOUSING SHORTAGE

The housing situation affects practically every branch of life. An acute shortage of teachers is being felt in Peeblesshire. One of the main reasons for this shortage is the difficulty new teachers find in obtaining suitable housing accommodation. The problem is almost insuperable. There seems nothing permanent that can be done to ease the problem.

South Midlothian Advertiser 2nd March 1945

ENEMY ALIENS

A protest that enemy aliens in Peebles were living a free and easy life, while returning servicemen were finding it a struggle to exist was made at the Annual General Meeting of the Peebles Branch of the British Legion. Mr. M... said it was the duty of the Legion to see that steps were taken to have those enemy aliens deported as soon as transport was available.

South Midlothian Advertiser 25th May 1945

EMPTY HOUSES SEIZED

Methods used by vigilantes and housing crusaders in seizing an empty house were described as "the law of the jungle" which could not be allowed to continue. The fact that families were homeless did not entitle them to steal other people's property.

Aberdeen Press and Journal 25th July 1945

POWs PREPARE BUILDING SITES

A recommendation that German prisoners of war be employed in the advance preparation of housing sites was heatedly discussed at the monthly meeting of the County Council.

Hamilton Advertiser 8th September 1945

ALL ELECTRIC HOUSES

A sub-Committee of the County Council recently met representatives of the Clyde Valley Electrical Power Company to discuss the possibility of erecting all-electric houses in the area served by the Company. A representative of the Company explained that it had been found that, on an average, the cost to the occupier of a four-apartment house within the Company's area was approximately £6.00 per annum.

Kirkintilloch Herald 5th November 1945

FIRST "PREFAB" HOUSES

Work on the first prefabricated houses to be erected in Scotland was started at Poltonhall last Friday. The

houses, 45 of which are to be built at this site, have walls with a heating resistance equal to $13\frac{1}{2}$" of brick. They are equipped with modern conveniences and have a special fireplace which will burn coal, anthracite or coke. In summer months, when a fire is not required, the water can be heated by electricity.

Dalkeith Advertiser 8th November 1945

PLASTICS

We stand at the doorway to an age of plastics. The extended use thereof is one of the few advantages that war has brought us. More and more will plastics be used in the home and naturally women will want to know about them. Mr. James Robson, Peebles, gave a talk on the new substances as adaptable to handicraft

Prefabs at Sutties Lea, Newtongrange.

and decorative work. He exhibited several examples of plasticwork including vases, decorative panels and ashtrays, the ash receptacle on the latter being fashioned from a seashell all of which were greatly admired.

South Midlothian Advertiser
23rd November 1945

PREFABS

The newcomers to the "land of Prefabrication" will want to know what sort of state they are entering and what they may expect when they are settled down in their new abodes. To begin with they should know that the houses are all of three apartments with kitchenette - living room and two bedrooms. Provision is made for a refrigerator in each home. These are not on the market at the moment but when peace time production gets into a swing in the factories they will emerge and make their appearance.

Motherwell Times 7th December 1945

Careful with that water heater...

it's **COAL** you're burning

The country's stocks of coal have still to be built up after a hard winter. The wheels of industry must still speed the war effort — they are driven by coal. Both gas and electricity come from coal, so use them with care and only when really necessary. Don't forget — watch that gas tap and guard that switch! Save fuel wherever you can every day.

CUT YOUR GAS & ELECTRICITY THEY BOTH COME FROM COAL!

CLASSES TOO LARGE

The view that it was a waste of time to talk about raising the school age if they did nothing to restrict the size of classes in Scottish schools was expressed at a special meeting of Stirling County Council to discuss the Education (Scotland) Bill.

The Council expressed disappointment that there was nothing in the Bill stipulating the size of classes a teacher was compelled to teach. They could not expect pupils to be educated while classes were as large as they were today. There was not much use in increasing the school age or to do many other things if they did not restrict the size of the classes so as to give the teacher and the pupils every opportunity.

Falkirk Herald 6th January 1945

PLANNING

The Town and Country Planning (Scotland) Bill has received a second reading in the Commons, but it cannot be said that it had an enthusiastic welcome from Scottish Members. The Bill deals primarily with the special problems of the blitzed areas, but it is the so-called blighted areas of Scotland that present much more formidable difficulties than anything the Germans have so far been able to create with their bombs.

Falkirk Herald 17th February 1945

VICTORY FARTHINGS

The Lothians Electric Power Company have announced a reduction in the domestic two-part tariff. This reduction of a quarter pence per unit may well be termed "victory farthings" and is a welcome contribution towards the post-war rehabilitation of our servicemen and women. It may be wondered how this reduction can be made in these days of increased costs for this, that and the next thing, and it says much for the outlook of private enterprise that this long-term policy and practical help is being given to housing development. While there is still the urgent necessity for economy in consumption till the coal situation improves, increased use of electricity by the ordinary consumer tends to reduce tariffs and the widespread adoption of "all-electric" houses has justified the present reduction.

Dalkeith Advertiser 22nd March 1945

SCHOOL ABSENTEEISM

Arising from the prosecution of defaulters for not complying with attendance orders pronounced against them in respect of the unsatisfactory school attendance of their children, correspondence has passed in the matter of the enforcement of the imprisonment penalty imposed as an alternative to the payment of fines.

It was the established practice to enforce the imprisonment penalty in cases of defaulters who had shown defiance, and there had been some hesitation in enforcing warrants in cases of defaulters who were widows or whose husbands were serving HM

Contributions...

No. 17   THE EARTH MOVERS

Scrapers, Graders, Tractors and numerous other types of vehicles used for " Bulldozing " in aerodrome construction and cultivation of land for food production had tyres by Dunlop.

by **DUNLOP**

Forces, especially where there were large young families.

Hamilton Advertiser 24th March 1945

BLOOD BANK

Bellshill Maternity Hospital which was one of the pioneers in blood transfusion service before the war, having at call a number of blood donors residing at convenient distance from the hospital, is now drawing supplies from the "blood bank" for Glasgow and West of Scotland.

Motherwell Times 10th August 1945

OUTLOOK BLACK

In statements made by Government spokesmen this week it has been made plain that no-one in Britain can look forward to a period of easy prosperity in the future. We have been warned by the Chancellor of the Exchequer against harbouring extravagant expectations of tax relief; we have been told that the changeover of industry from war production to a peace basis will involve some temporary unemployment; we have been informed that the resettlement of servicemen in civilian employment following demobilisation and the erection of the homes needed to house them will call for prodigious efforts, and we have learned that stringent economies in food, fuel and clothing are as necessary today as at any period during the war.

Inverness Courier 24th August 1945

COAL

Nationalisation of the coal fields would ensure not only an improvement in the conditions of mineworkers throughout the country, but would be of inestimable benefit to every other industry in Great Britain declared Miss Margaret Herbison, Labour M.P. for North Lanark. Miss Herbison said that not only had this country suffered from a coal shortage during the past six years, due to the fact that coal was required for war purposes, but the shortage was also aggravated by the fact that coalowners were reserving the best seams for competitive overseas trade.

Kirkintilloch Herald 29th August 1945

NO UNEMPLOYMENT

We confess we are at a loss to understand why fears should be entertained about mass unemployment in Britain. Apart from the work of rebuilding our own bombed cities and the rehousing and reconstruction which everybody is agreed are post-war priorities, there is bound to be a tremendous demand all over the world for everything we can produce. There should be no unemployment in Britain after demobilisation - that is, provided the Government takes steps to see that the raw materials which British industry urgently requires are forthcoming.

Inverness Courier 11th September 1945

HEALTH EDUCATION

A novel and interesting venture in the field of health education has been set afoot by the Scottish Council for Health Education.

The Council recently appointed Dr. J. N. Greene Nolan (a psychiatrist invalided out of the R.A.M.C. who has a wide medical experience both at home and abroad) as a medical lecturer to accompany the cinemotor van on a six months tour of the rural and highland areas of Scotland.

Thousands of people - men, women and children - have heard "pep" talks on such subjects as sleep, fatigue, worry, childhood fears, care of the feet...and so on and have seen many remarkable films.

Dalkeith Advertiser 22nd November 1945

NATIONALISATION

Mr. Morrison's announcement of the Government's five-year plan of nationalisation took the Opposition by surprise and has been the main topic of conversation in the lobbies and smoke-rooms this week.

Hamilton Advertiser 24th December 1945

The long struggle for the ownership of the coalmines, which has time and again convulsed industry, seems in a fair way to ending at last. The miners have had their way. The Coal Industry Nationalisation Bill, published on the day Parliament adjourned for Christmas is a Bill to acquire the British coal mines for the State.

Hamilton Advertiser 29th December 1945

Waiting to collect coal.

Here he is—Symbolic of the young men who are stepping out of War ready to take a place in bringing the Country back to normal conditions. He is thankful to be back—so, too, is the Nation, and the best way to show our gratitude for what he has done can be expressed by Saving. In this way we can help him to re-establish his position and help along the plans that mean better Housing—Health—Happiness.

GIVE THANKS BY SAVING

Bring in **THE VICTORY HARVESTS—VOLUNTEERS WANTED**

 3,000 SENIOR SCHOOL GIRLS ARE NEEDED FOR THE FRUIT PICKING

 12,000 MEN and WOMEN FROM OFFICES AND FACTORIES **FOR THE GRAIN HARVEST**

 61,000 BOYS and GIRLS (12 years and over) TO HELP WITH THE POTATO LIFTING

The food is in the fields —you are needed there too!

Children should seek information from their schools.

VOLUNTEERS FOR THE GRAIN HARVEST (MID-AUGUST AND SEPTEMBER) ARE INVITED TO FILL UP THIS COUPON FOR DETAILS.

Send me by return, postage-paid enrolment form and leaflet which explains the Harvest Help Scheme in detail, including hostel accommodation, wages, transport facilities, etc.

Name, _____

Address, _____

_____

B.7

·········· CUT OUT AND POST TO ··········

THE DEPARTMENT OF AGRICULTURE FOR SCOTLAND, 15 GROSVENOR STREET, EDINBURGH, 12

"Children are introduced to their cultural heritage and are helped to compare and contrast their life with that of people in other times. They begin to understand some of the ways in which the past can be reconstructed through the use of source material and to appreciate the importance of evidence and its use in making judgement about events."

Learning and Teaching:
The Environment and the Primary School Curriculum.
Scottish Education Department. 1984.

"Historians employ a range of skills which help to define their discipline.
Using and analysing a range of source materials.
Pupils should be helped to analyse both primary evidence and secondary accounts and to detect, in particular, omissions, the personal standpoint of past writers and the use of emotive or figurative language..."

History from 5 to 16. Curriculum Matters No. 11. Department
of Education and Science. 1988

The above quotations demonstrate the importance of source material in pupils' involvement with what has been called exploration of their past environment. Use of historical sources was traditionally regarded as an activity conducted at a relatively high level, demanding both advanced inferential skills and the necessity to place what was inferred in the context of previous knowledge and understanding.

Of late however, good language teaching, including such activities as cloze procedure and prediction exercises, combined with an ever increasing sophistication in thematic studies at upper primary and secondary level, have enabled the explanation (and subsequent communication) of "first hand" texts to take their place alongside observation and recording in an active methodology. To provide a Scotland-wide collection of newspaper sources, focused on a particular year of considerable interest, and capable of producing a range of responses at individual and group level, is a major purpose of this book.

The responses to these glimpses of fifty years ago will vary. Each of the sections in itself could form part of the evidence for an in-depth era study, or it could add a "Scottish Dimension" to an examination of the last months of war and the first months of peace, or it could simply furnish the material for a dramatic presentation "Our Town in 1945". A more complete list of suggested responses is appended.

SOME ACTIVITIES

1.   FINDING THE MAIN IDEA or identification of specific themes or main ideas which appear throughout the extracts. Options for activities in this area include group discussion designed to reach a consensus on what the main idea consists of, headline writing (or where a headline is provided, discussion on appropriateness), prediction exercises, general discussion of issues such as propaganda. (Are there examples in the book? What were the reasons given? Do you think they were justified?)

2.   COMPARISON/CONTRAST. Pupils could examine features of life in 1945 and draw comparisons and contrasts with the contemporary scene. A range of possibilities presents itself such as improvised or scripted dramatisations of situations then and now, e.g. Shopping and Food, Government and Council Regulations, Work, the Role of Women, Housing, Health & Welfare.

3.   LOCAL STUDIES

a)   Fieldwork. Some activities could be connected with 2 above, for example investigating the present condition of places mentioned in the text, making direct comparison with the written description, or with old photographs and maps, producing video or slide/tape presentations of findings.

b)   Making particular use of human resources.   With luck, tracing individuals mentioned in the text, or their descendants. Collecting reminiscences and interviewing, making attempts to discover different perspectives on events; all are possibilities.

c)   Making general use of human resources.   As above, talking to and obtaining information from members of generations who lived through 1945. Interviews could select different aspects of the text and raise questions like "Was it really like this?"

4.   OTHER IDEAS

Some ways of using the sources include: the annotation by pupils of the source using photocopied pages, the notes being written, graphic or a combination of both; collating and presenting the notes in a tabular form so as to encourage classification and generalisation; examining paired sources or a series of sources; presenting the conclusions from this activity; extracting and organising different forms of information under headings like "How did people ensure there was enough food to go round?".

A key question relating to the use of this particular kind of source is: "Is the source being used in the context of some background knowledge or is the pupil expected to draw inferences from the source itself?"   Both approaches have merits but the teacher will wish to be clear about the purpose when setting the assignment.

The knowledge and understanding to be gained might be organised as follows:

- similarities and differences between the experience of men, women and children

- the scale of the organisation and administration required to sustain the war effort and post-war reconstruction

- ways in which public awareness and morale were awakened

- the cost, human and material, of the war

- specific ideas and concepts e.g. the atomic bomb

5.   POSSIBLE USE OF THE BOOK IN RELATION TO PERSONAL AND SOCIAL DEVELOPMENT

Some of the entries or "sources" in the book might lead teachers and pupils to consider and reflect upon a wide range of forms of human experience.   In turn, this reflection could lead on to imaginative and creative responses in the form of presentations of, for example:

- experiences of loss, grief and suffering

- hopes and fears

- the meaning of sacrifice

- reasons for celebration and remembrance

- experiences of community, collaboration and sharing of values

- fresh starts, regeneration and new beginnings.

Ronald Armstrong